MAZE
ADVENTURES

Rf

F

Escaping from mazes is fiendishly difficult...but it's lots of fun to try!
See if you can find some mazes you can explore near your home.

Draw Your Own Maze
You'll find instructions at the back of this book and more information
on the website. Share your creations and maze adventures with us
on our Facebook page or on Twitter using the hashtag #bsmallmazes.
Our details are below.

If you have enjoyed this book, look out for other
creative activity books from b small publishing. Join us online at:
www.bsmall.co.uk
www.facebook.com/bsmallpublishing
@bsmallbear

Published by b small publishing ltd.
www.bsmall.co.uk
English translation © b small publishing ltd. 2013
Original text and illustrations © Hurra Forlag as
Monolitveien 12, 0375 Oslo, Norway
arranged through books&rights

1 2 3 4 5

Printed in China by WKT Co. Ltd.

ISBN: 978-1-908164-69-8

British Library Cataloguing-in-Publication Data.
A catalogue record for this book is available from the British Library.

MAZE ADVENTURES

There's only one way out!

by Martin Nygaard
illustrated by Jesús Gabán

b small publishing

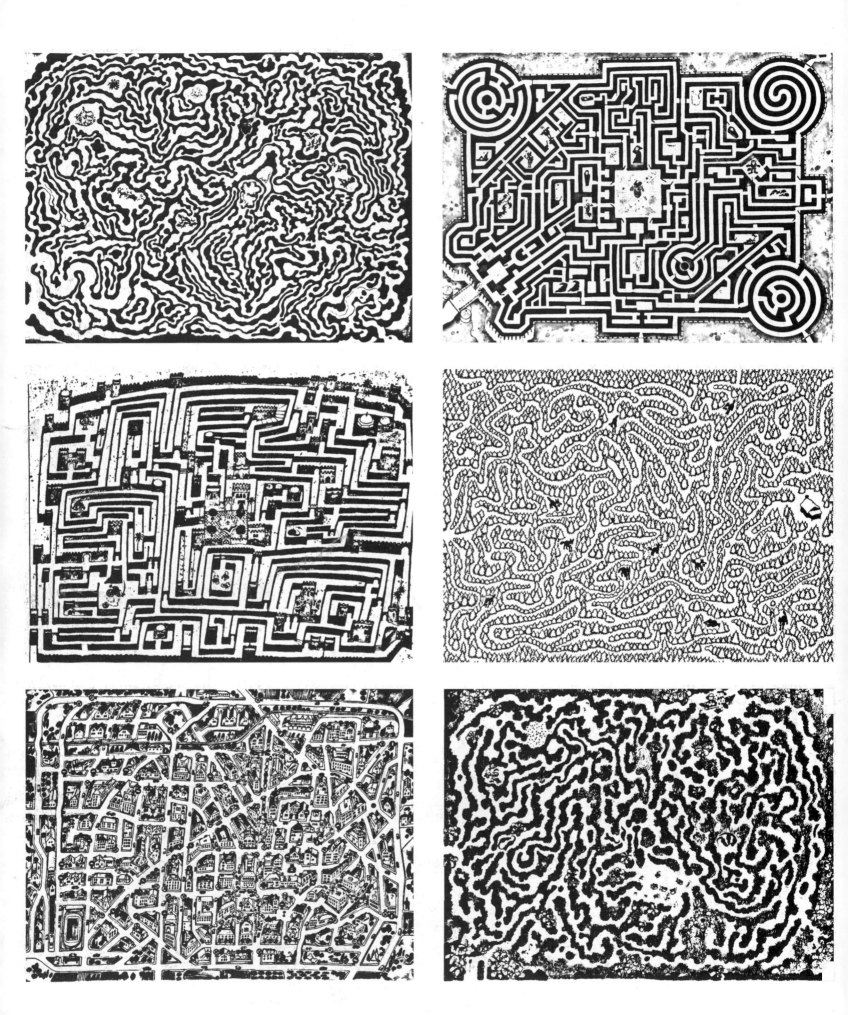

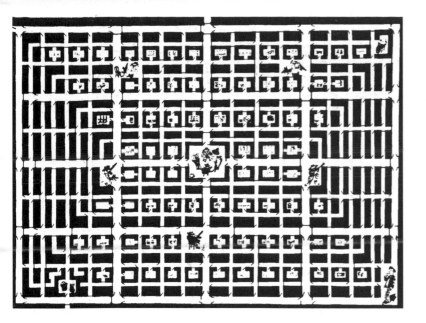

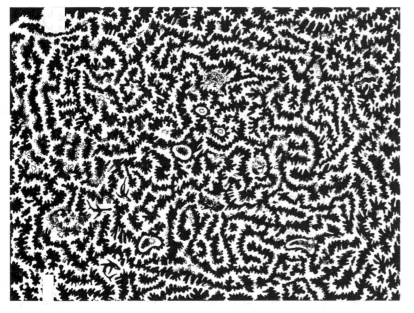
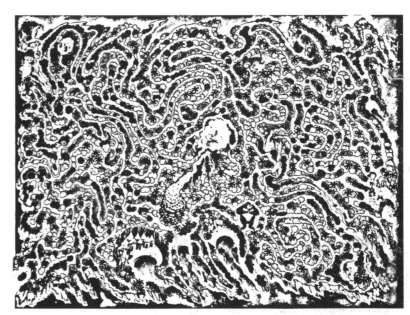
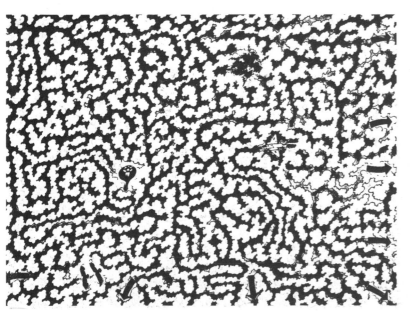

CAVE OF WONDERS

Jack and Jessica are bravely hunting for hidden treasure. They're deep in a mountain cave. But what's that hiding in the darkness?

There are rabid rats, vampire bats, seas of molten lava and a HUGE deadly spider...

'I think you'd better turn on your head torch, Jessica,' says Jack with a shaky voice, 'or who knows what we'll bump into.'

Jessica shivers. 'It looks very scary,' she says. 'Can someone help us find our way through?'

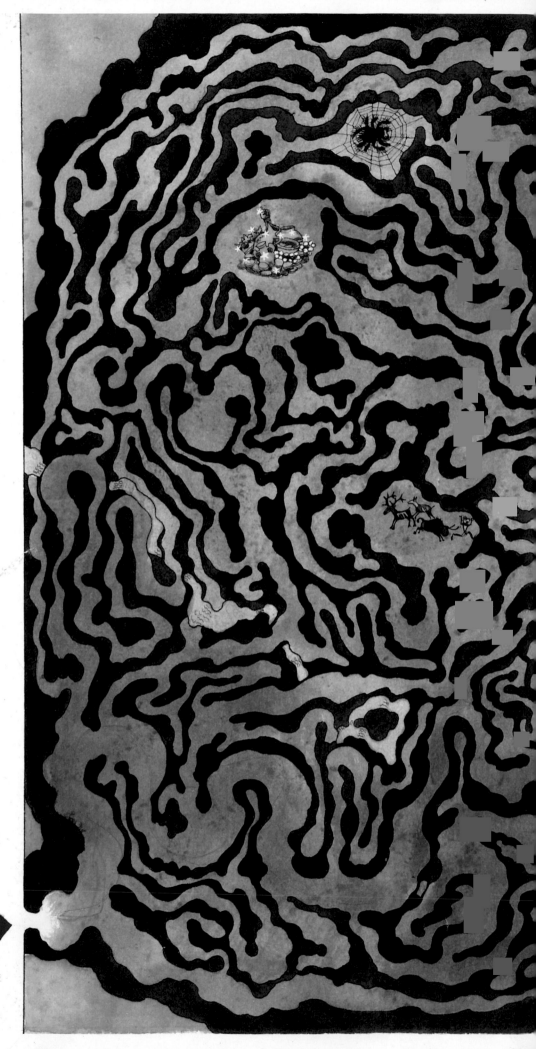

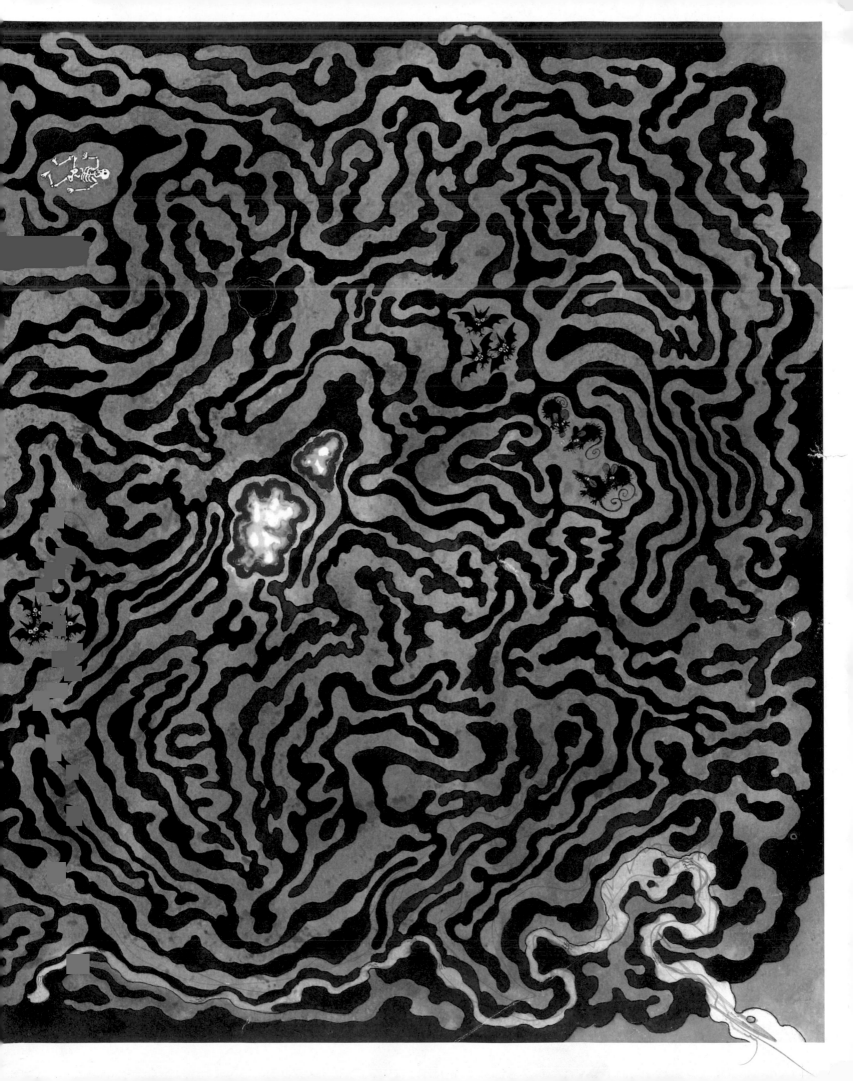

THE HAUNTED CASTLE

As they emerge safely from the mountain, a terrible storm breaks. Jack and Jessica race out of the rain and into a big castle.

The door slams behind them...and it's stuck fast. The sound of a witch cackling in the darkness stops them dead in their tracks. Jack jumps at the sound of an old chest creaking open and shut. Chains rattle from far across the castle.

'We need to get out of here NOW!' Jack whispers.

'Yes,' Jessica nods urgently, 'but which way?'

THE MIRAGE

The two friends stumble out of the haunted castle and begin to cross a sandy desert. They've been walking for days when they finally see the walls of a desert town.

Jack can hear running water and imagines a fresh pool of drinking water and lush, green trees with deep, cool shade. But he can't see the many dangers over the walls.

Can you help them find the refreshing fountain without falling into any pits? Watch out for the lion, snake, scorpion and evil-looking genie, too!

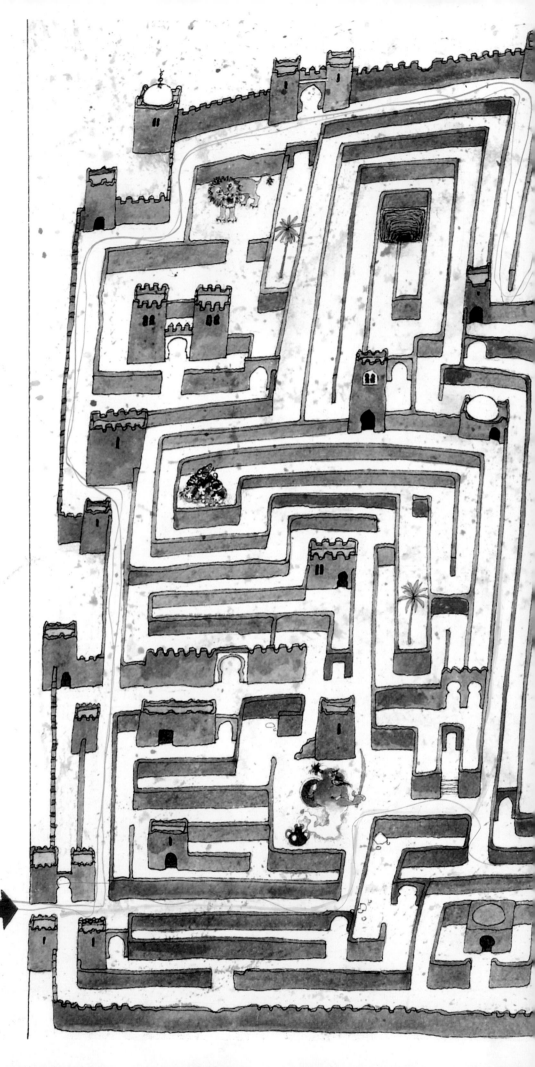

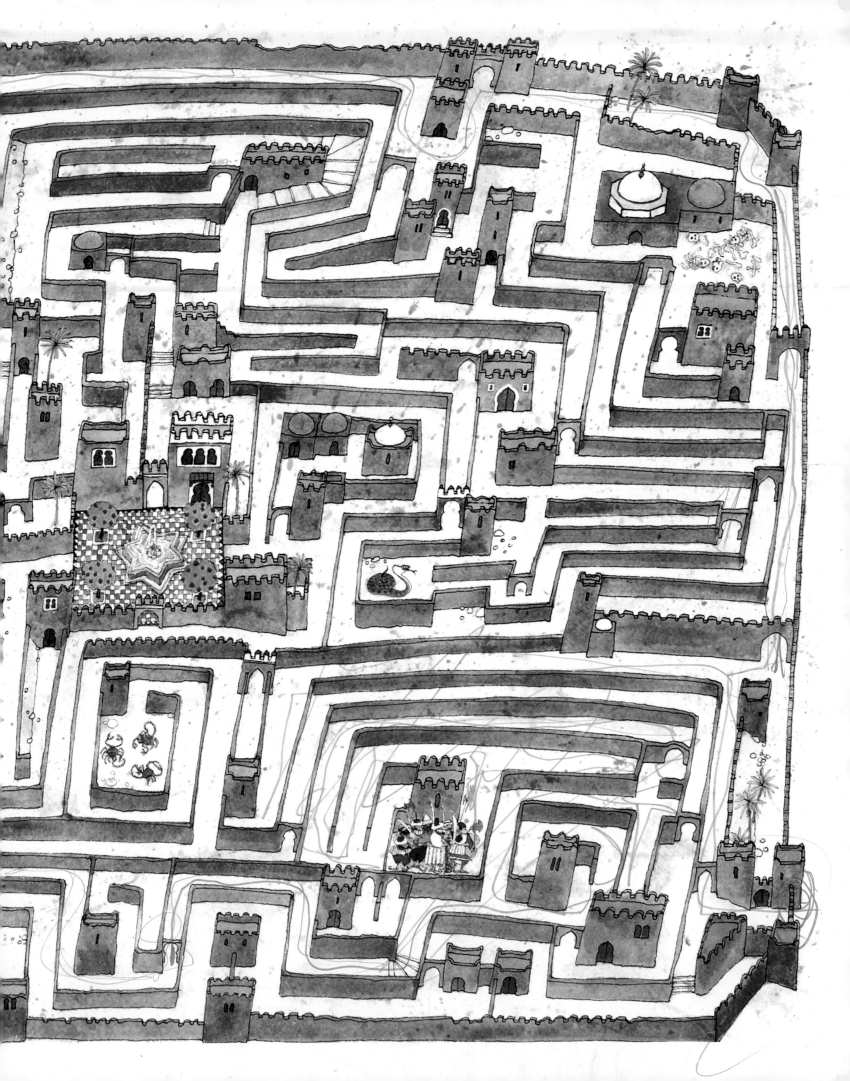

THE CABIN IN THE SNOW

Now Jack and Jessica head to the Arctic. The trees of the forest all look the same covered in snow. If they can find their way to the little cabin, they'll have shelter for the night.

Jack leads the way on his skis. More snow starts to fall thick and fast. The smoke from the cabin's chimney slowly disappears into the darkness and the wolves start to howl.

Can you help them reach the warm cabin safely?

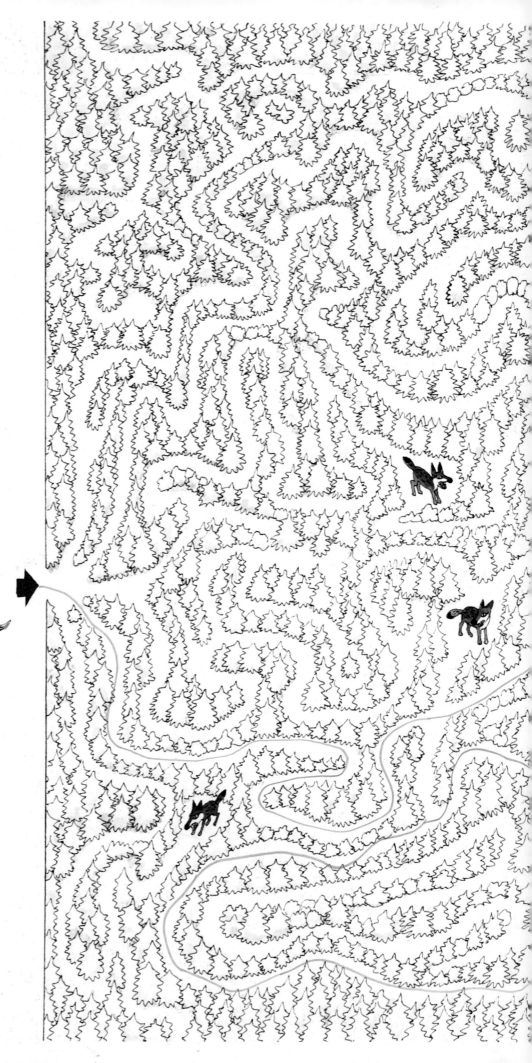

A FUNNY TURN

The adventures continue! But the food in that cabin seems to have made them both ill. They'd better find a chemist quickly.

'The roads in this town are a nightmare,' grumbles Jessica. 'It's full of one-way streets, no left or right turns, roadworks, barriers and so much traffic!'

'If we don't find that chemist, we'll have a bad night, Jessica,' groans Jack.

No entry

No right turn

Chemist

ADVENTURES IN THE AMAZON

Next stop for Jack and Jessica - the Amazon in Brazil!

'All we need to do is follow the route marked on that map I gave you,' says Jessica.

Jack looks worried as he slowly reaches for his rucksack.

"What map...?' he asks sheepishly.

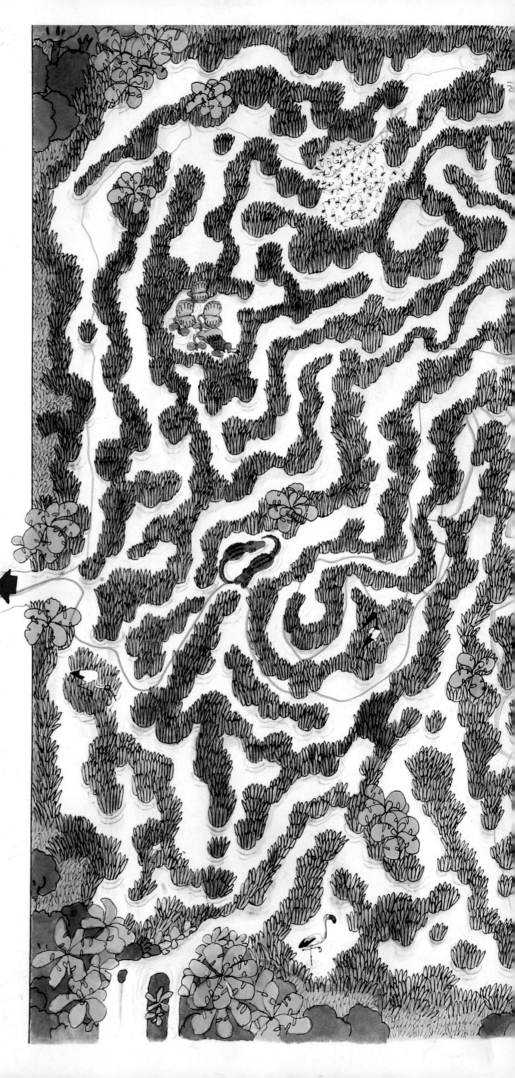

Jessica rolls her eyes as Jack peers into the water. They've heard a lot about the plants that can digest humans, the big crocodiles and the snapping piranha fish. Can you help them safely through?

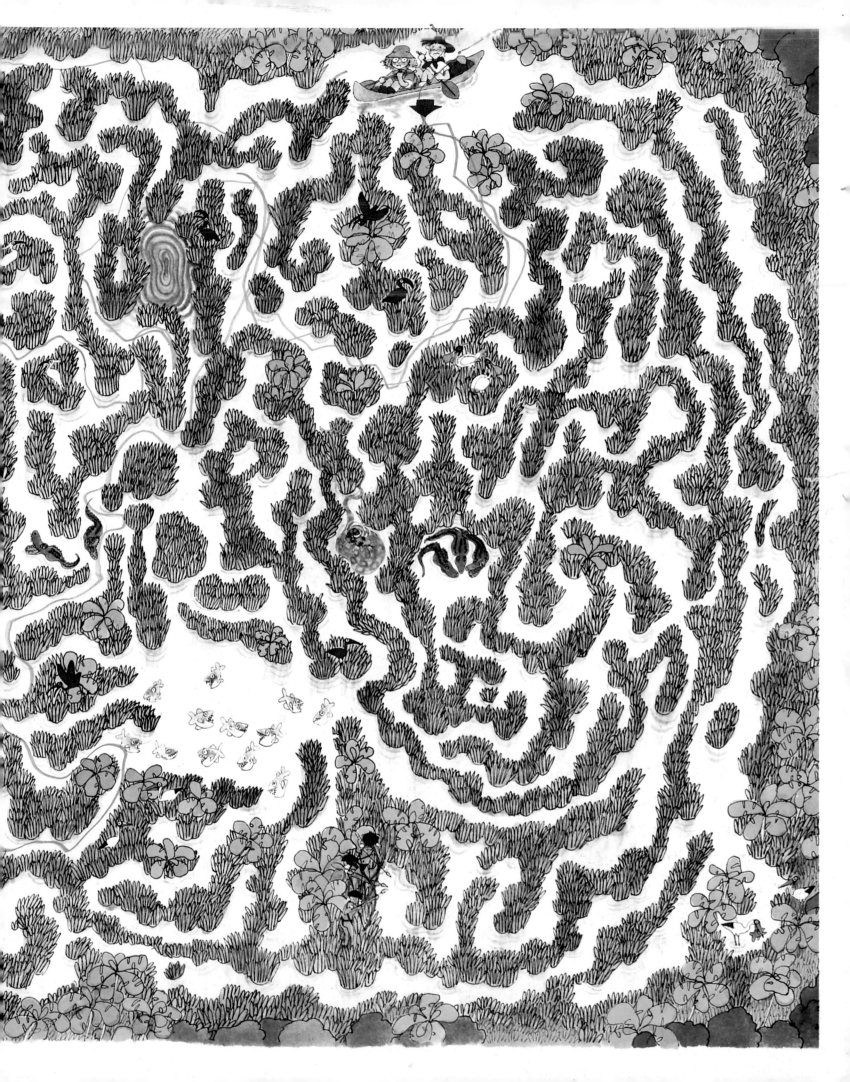

THE DARK CELLAR

Back in the city, Jessica is waiting outside the cinema. Jack is late and he has the tickets.

Jack doesn't want them to miss the film so he takes a shortcut. He races down the stairs and under the buildings. He rushes past the storerooms. He thinks he knows the way.

He can hear talking in the distance and sees someone in the darkness. The cellar is full of criminals!

Can you help him safely through the cellar to meet Jessica?

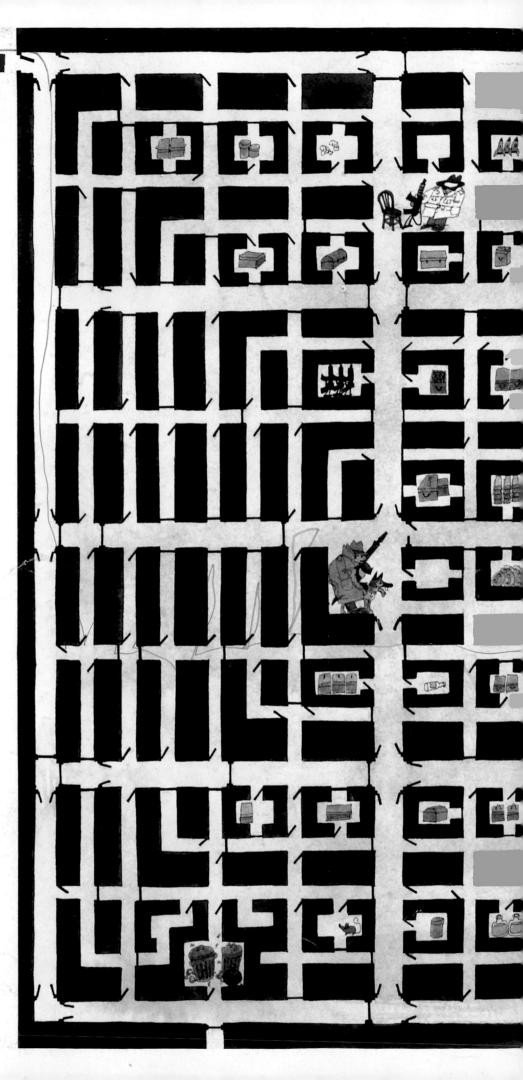

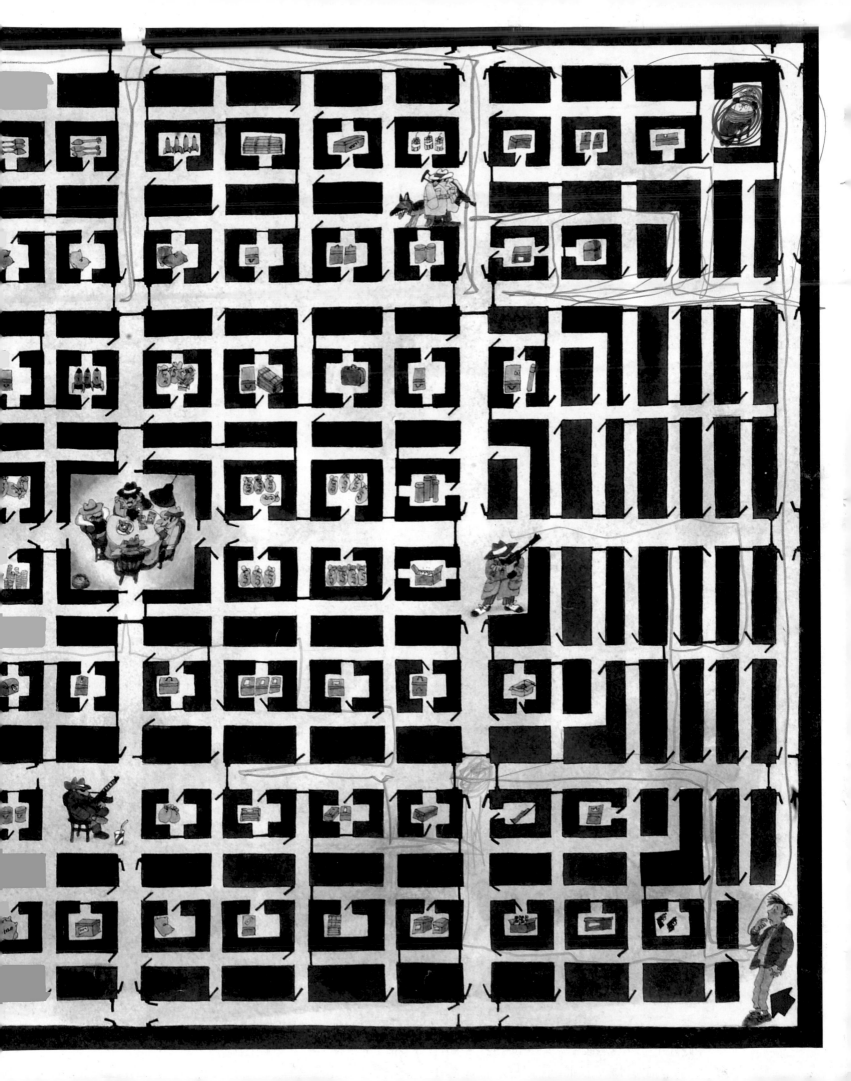

IN THESEUS' FOOTSTEPS

Jack had a chilly time in that cellar and he and Jessica saw a scary film. Now he's finding it hard to sleep. In his dreams he twists and turns through maze after maze until he finds himself in Ancient Greece! He's at the entrance to the Minotaur's Labyrinth.

Theseus conquered the Minotaur in his Labyrinth but Jack just wants to find his way out without meeting the bloodthirsty creature.

Can you help Jack out of this nightmare?

SHARK-INFESTED WATERS

The friends have heard about a galleon full of gold. It sank among the rocks in these dangerous waters. They want to find the treasure. They buy some diving equipment and swim out through the coral.

Many dangers lurk along the way. Help them to avoid the hungry sharks, the giant squid and the electric eel.

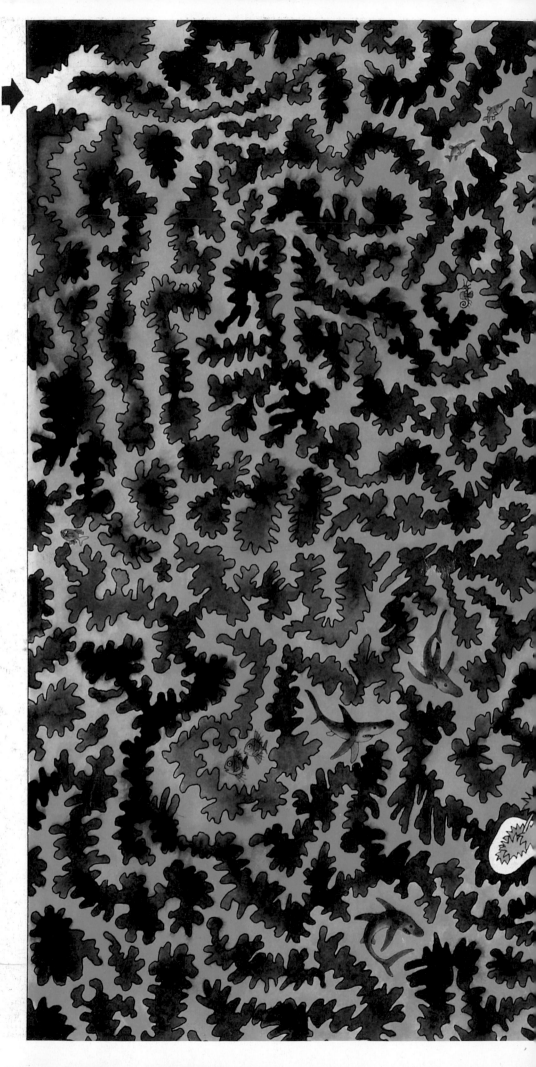

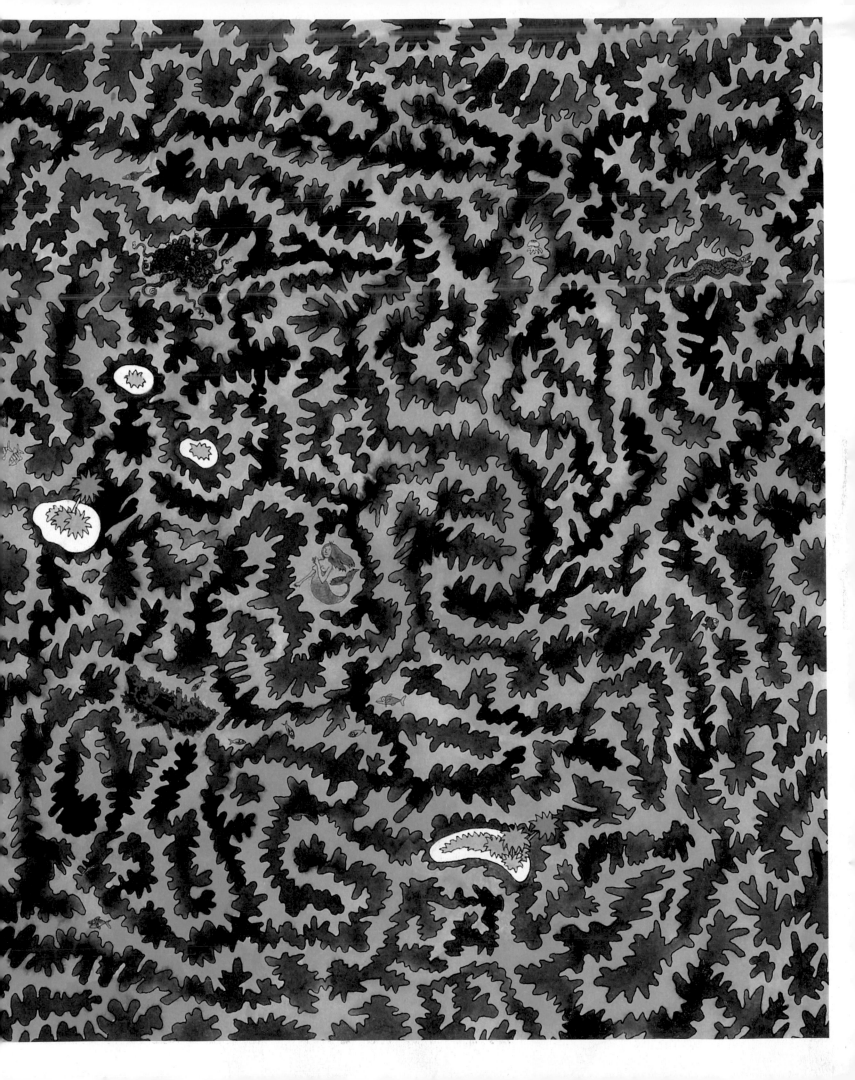

JURASSIC ISLAND

They found the gold and now they're rich! They've sailed their new boat to a luxury island in the middle of the ocean.

'We've been walking for ages! I don't think this is where we left the boat,' says Jessica. 'Let's have a swim in the ocean before we try to find our way back.'

There are so many trees on the island that they can't see a huge dinosaur, an active volcano, a ferocious tiger and even King Kong himself.

Can you help them back to their boat?

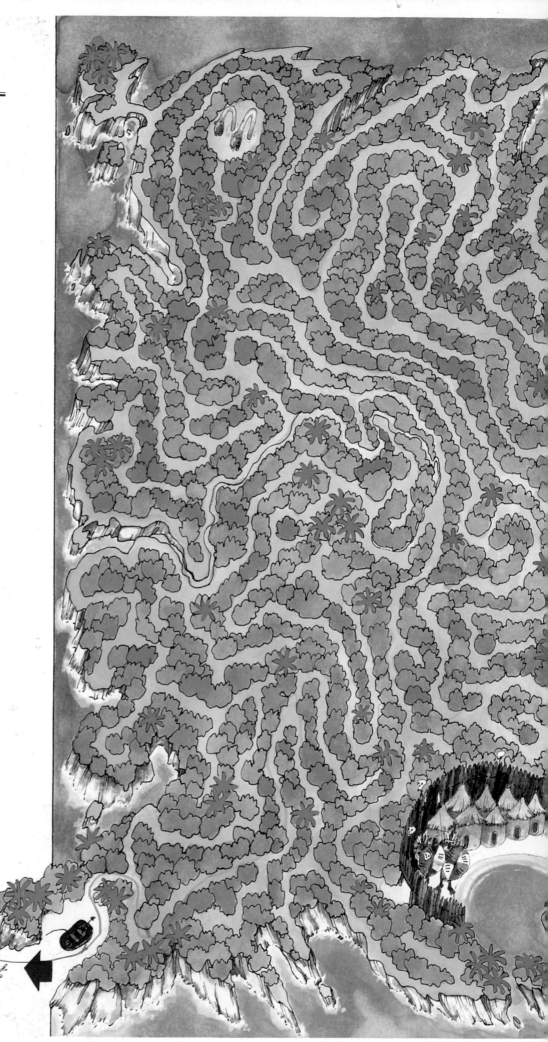

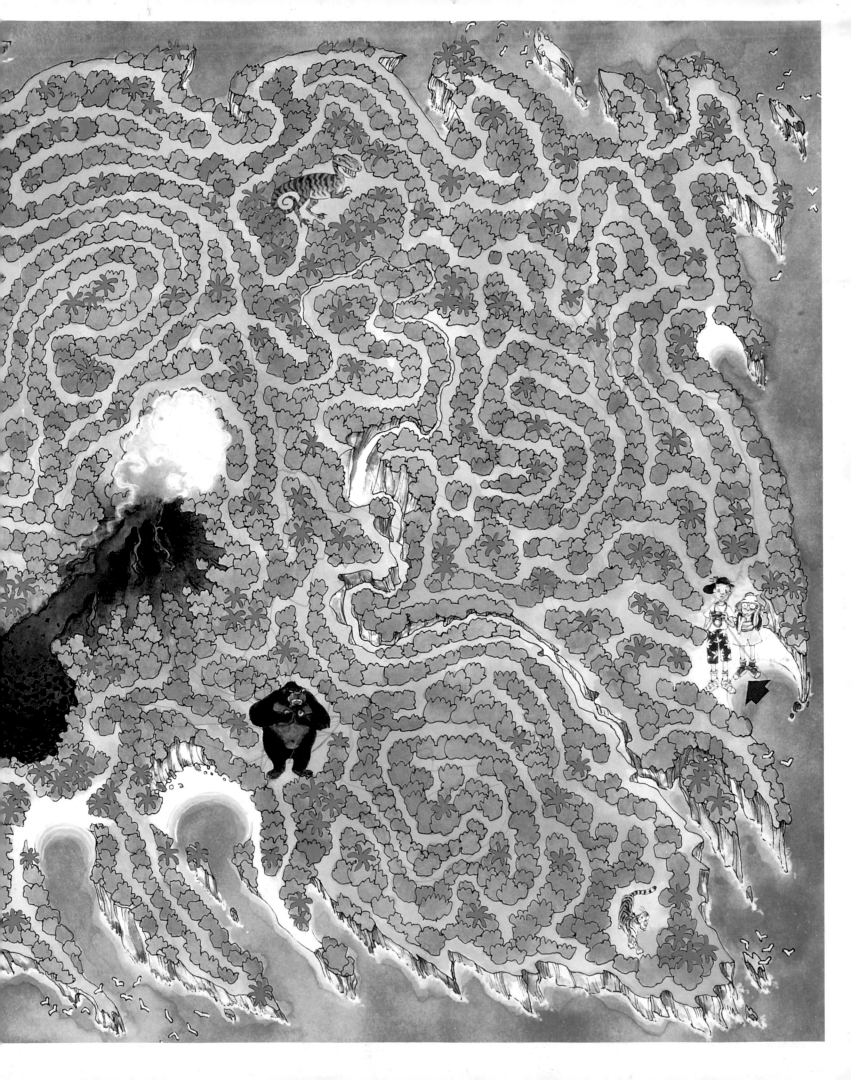

UP IN THE CLOUDS

Jack and Jessica are trying to fly home in a wreck of a plane. Their old plane can't cope with the clouds.

They're in danger of crashing into a hot air balloon, some hungry vultures, a fighter plane and a violent thunderstorm.

'We're low on fuel, Jessica,' Jack points out, 'we can't keep flying around for ever.'

'It's not exactly easy flying this old bucket,' Jessica replies without taking her eyes off the sky.

Can you lead them home through the maze of clouds?

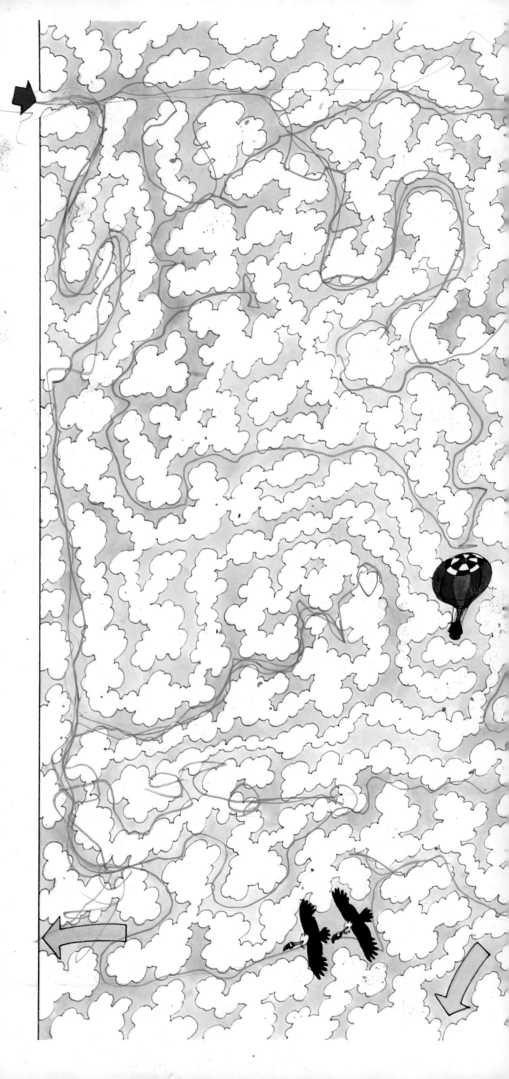

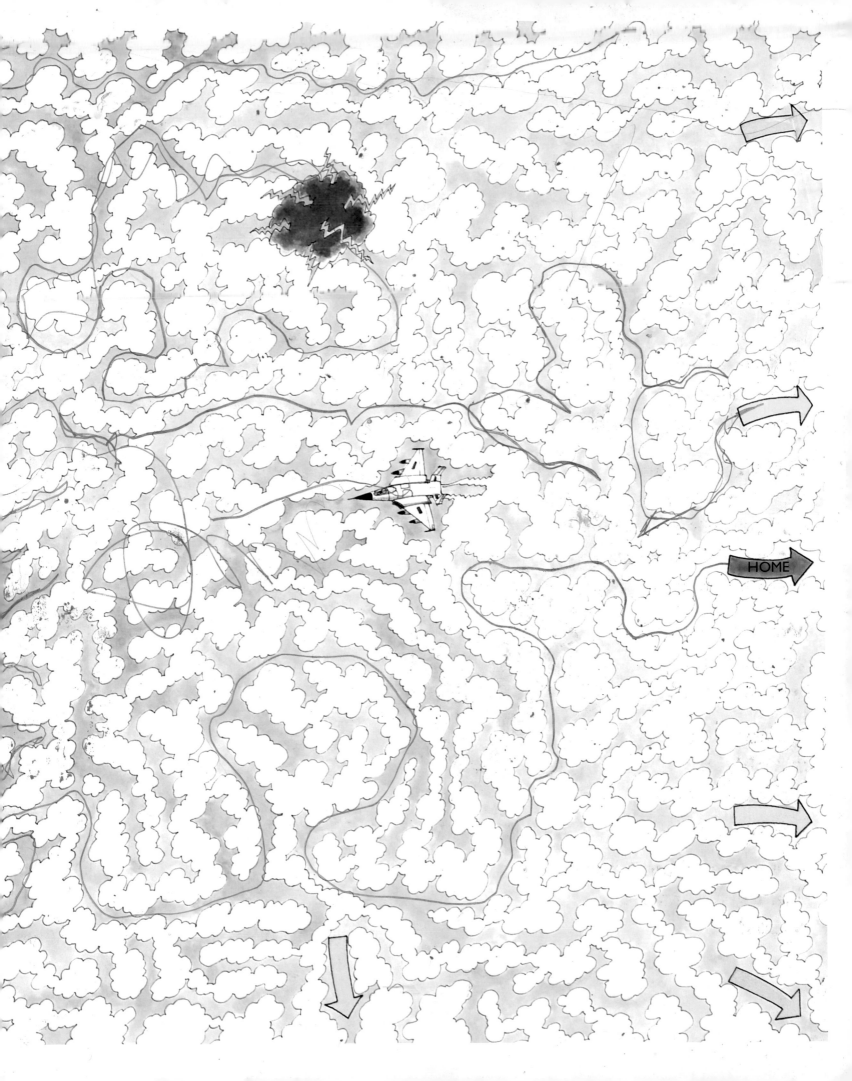

SPAGHETTI JUNCTION

Jessica landed the plane safely. They're nearly home! They're exhausted from their travels. But what do they find? Builders at the station have removed all the signs, the loudspeaker has broken so there are no announcements and the information desk is closed!

They live in Eastown. How will they get back to their home?

'We'll never work out which train we need,' sighs Jack.

'Someone will help us,' says Jessica. 'After all, they helped us through all our other adventures.'

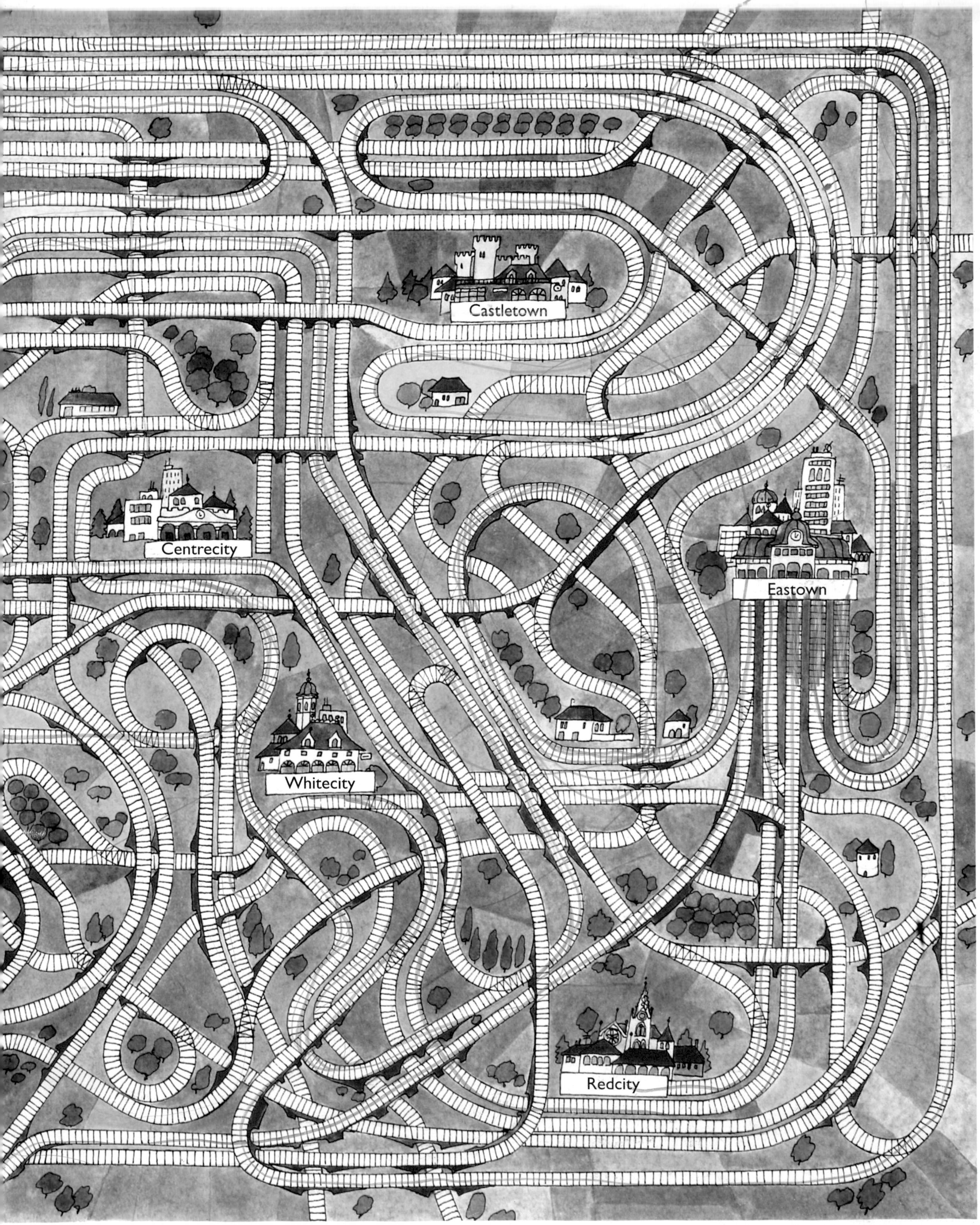
Castletown
Centrecity
Eastown
Whitecity
Redcity

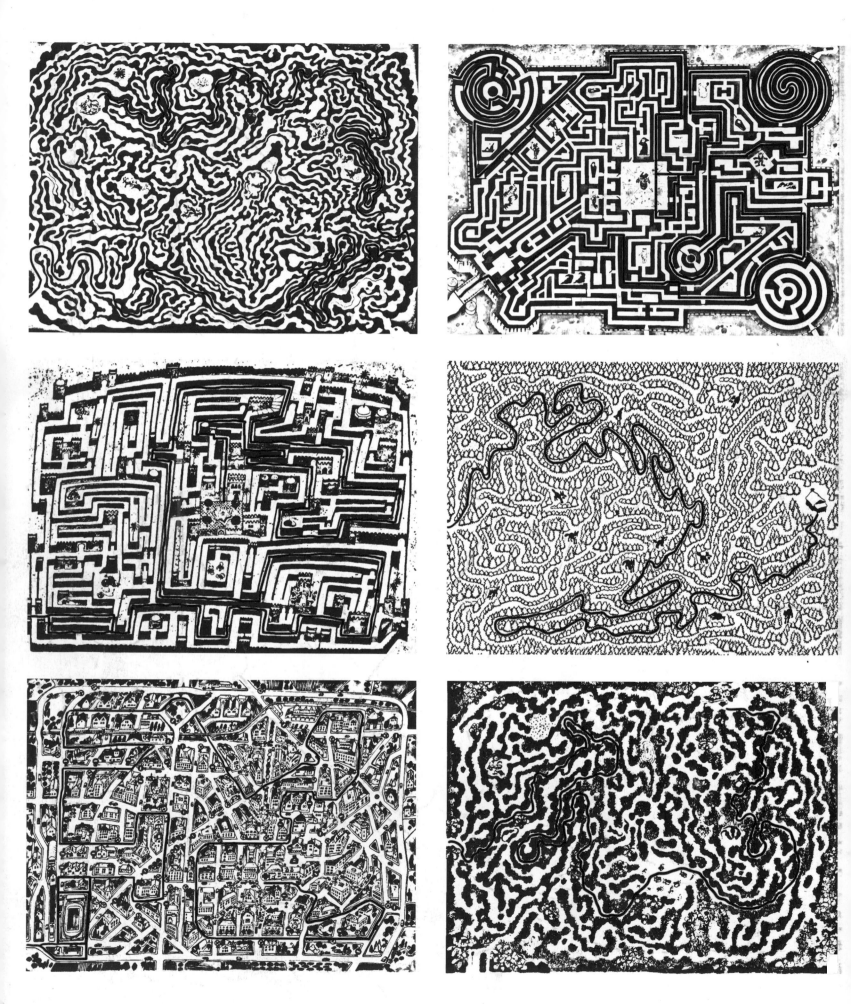

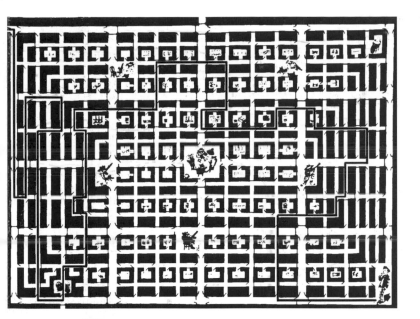

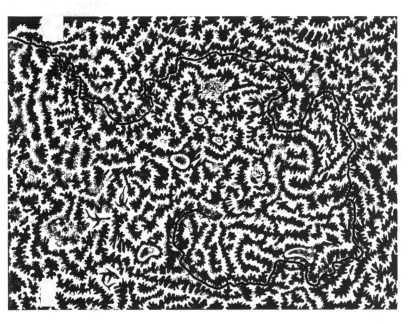

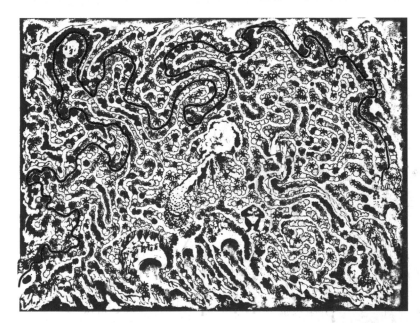

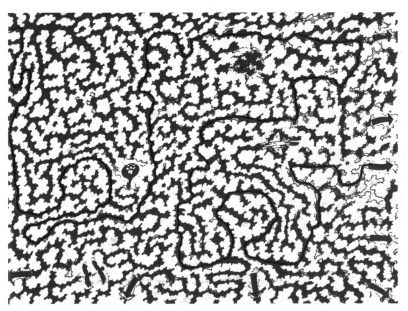

Make Your Own Maze!

You can make your own simple maze in a few easy steps. As you practise your maze-making skills, you'll be able to start making more and more difficult ones. You could even add tricks, traps and terrible dangers to make your maze exciting and challenging. Once you've created your maze, share it with us on Facebook or Twitter using the hashtag #bsmallmazes. Swap your creations with your friends and family to see if they can find their way out!

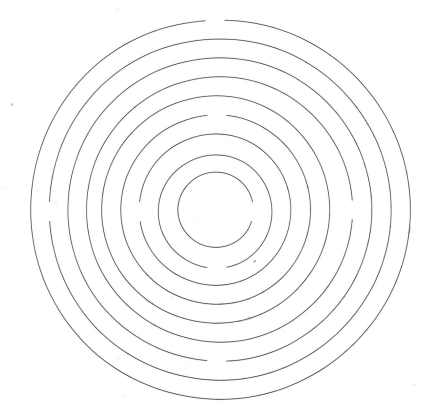

This is a very simple maze made by drawing one big circle then a smaller circle inside it and so on. Use a pencil so that you can then rub out doorways and make a pathway. You can make a maze using squares, rectangles, triangles – any shape! Why not try mixing shapes up? Just make sure that you provide a way in and a way out!

www.facebook.com/bsmallpublishing
@bsmallbear

b small publishing
www.bsmall.co.uk